PHARMACIST
COLORING BOOK

THIS BOOK BELONGS TO:

___

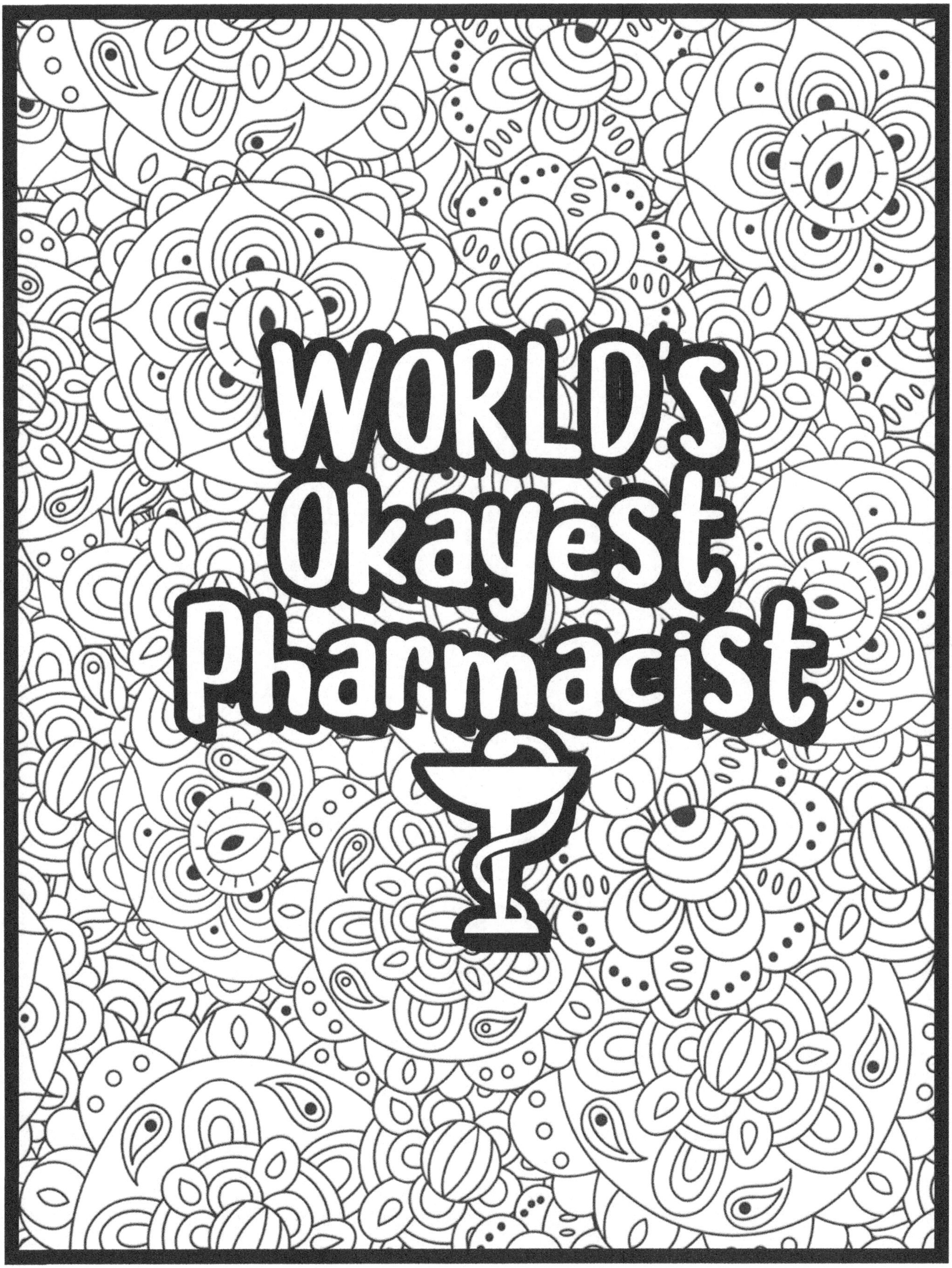
WORLD'S
Okayest
Pharmacist

WHEN LIFE
GIVES YOU
MOLD
MAKE
Penicillin

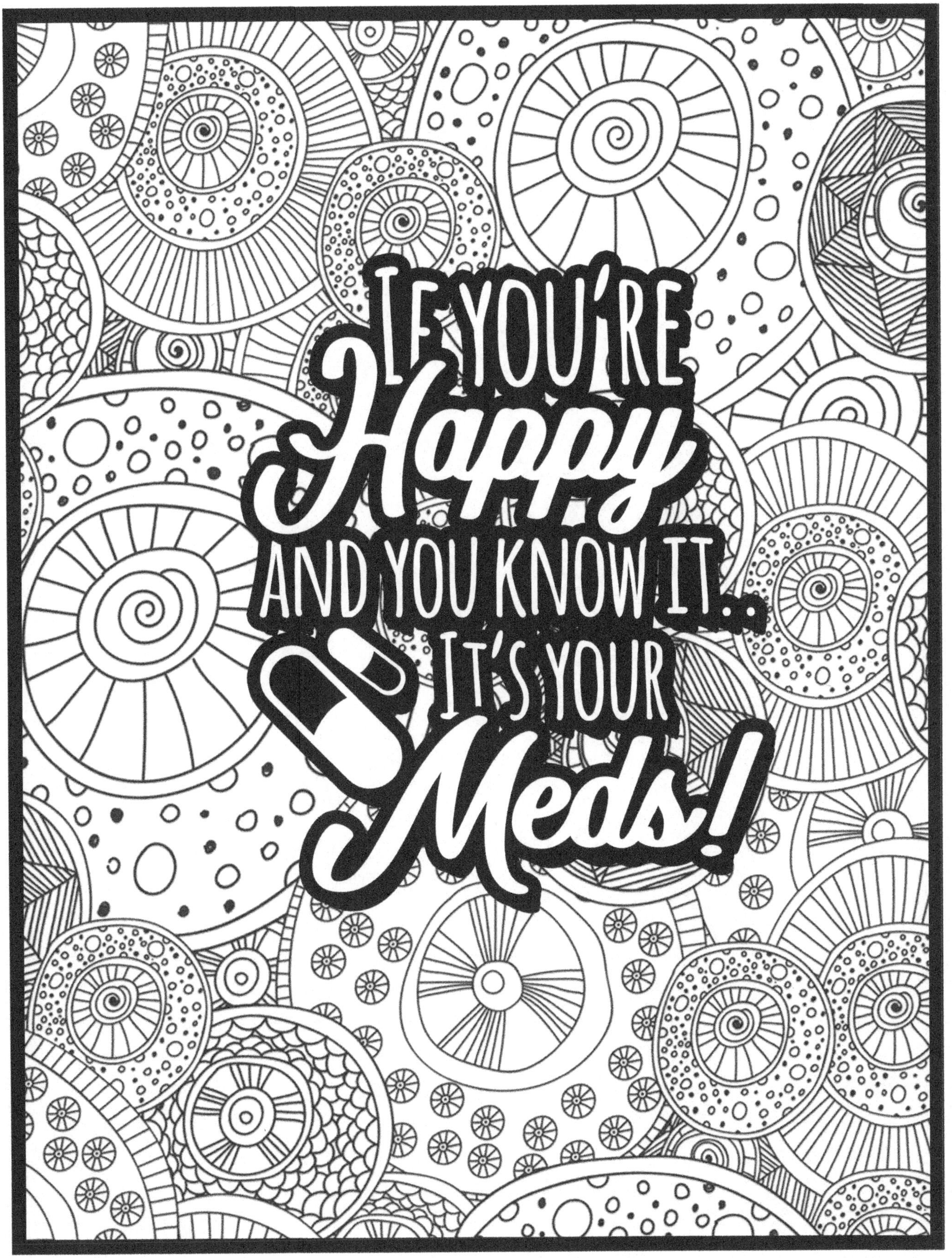
If you're
Happy
and you know it...
It's your
Meds!

PHARMACIST.
HEALER.
LEGEND.

LET THAT
SH!T Go!

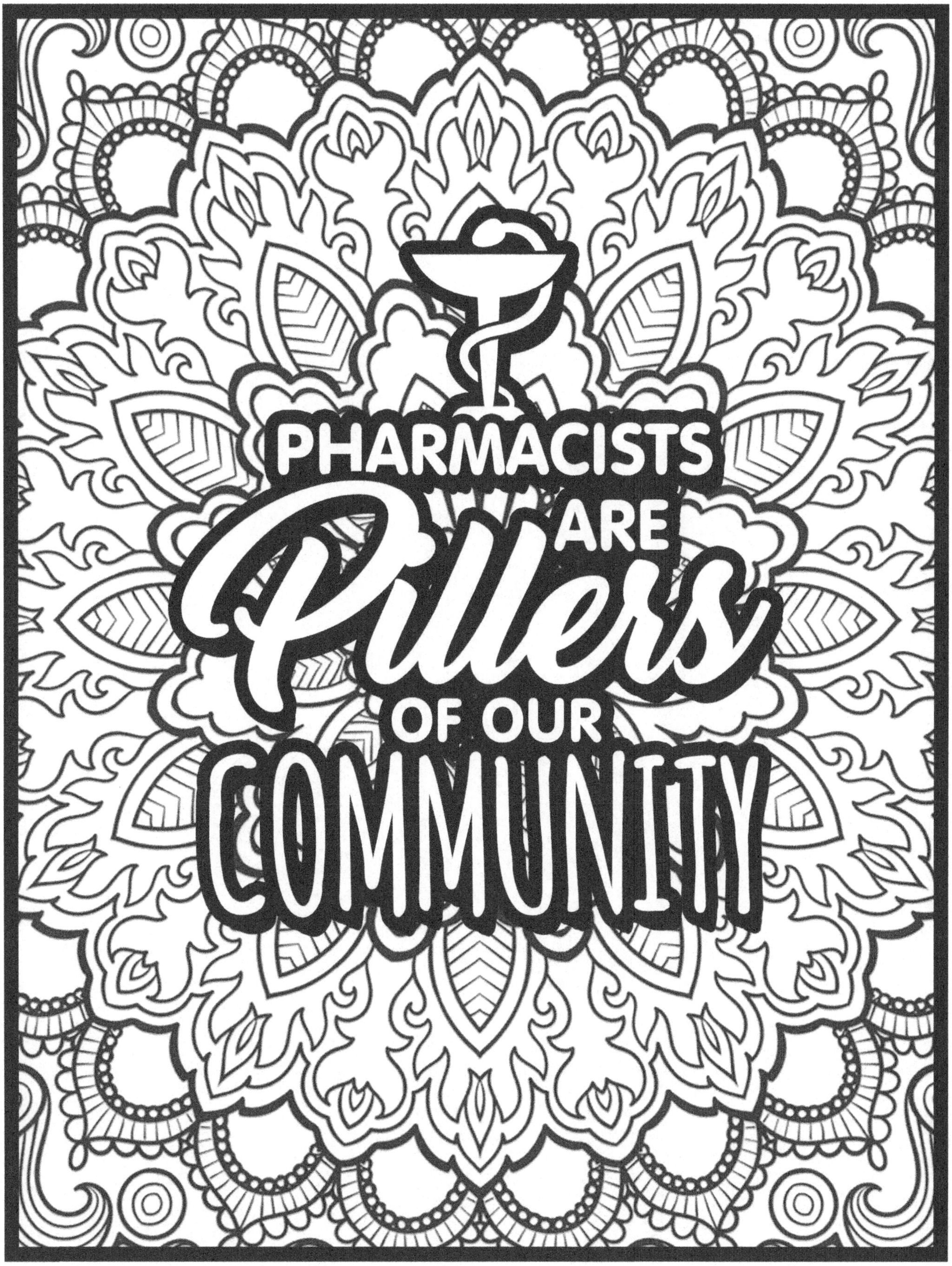
PHARMACISTS
ARE
Pillers
OF OUR
COMMUNITY

IF I DON'T MOVE FAST
PEOPLE WILL HAVE THE CHANCE TO ASK ME THINGS!

I SUFFER
FROM
RESTING
PHARMACIST
FACE

ABSOLUTELY
F*CKING

What
the
Actual
FUCK
?

It's What it Fucking is

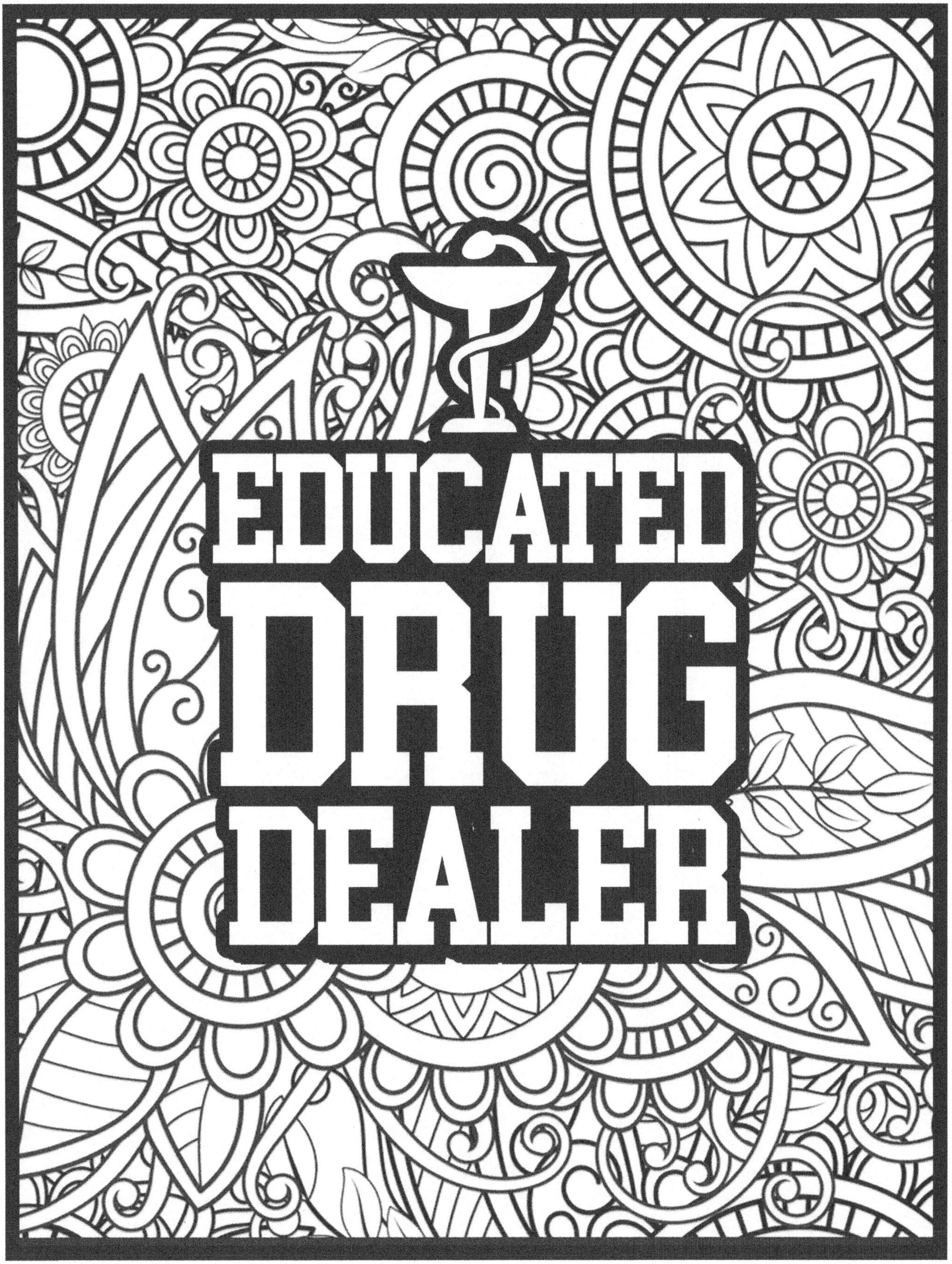
EDUCATED
DRUG
DEALER

GOOD MORNING
DOCTOR
UNFORTUNATELY
WE DON'T HAVE
SCRIBBLE
IN STOCK

STAYS LATE
TO FILL Rx
PATIENT
WENT
SHOPPING

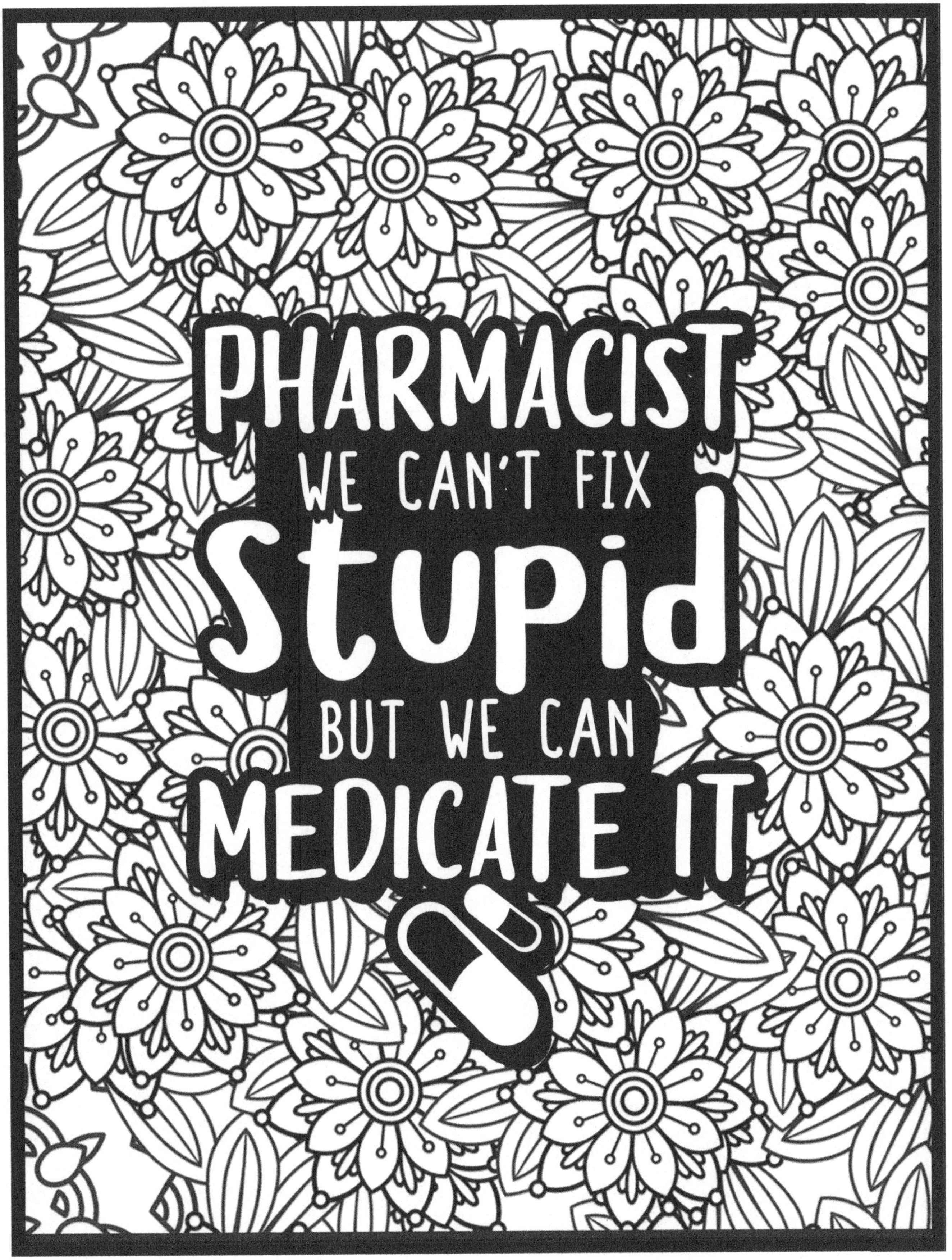
PHARMACIST
WE CAN'T FIX
Stupid
BUT WE CAN
MEDICATE IT

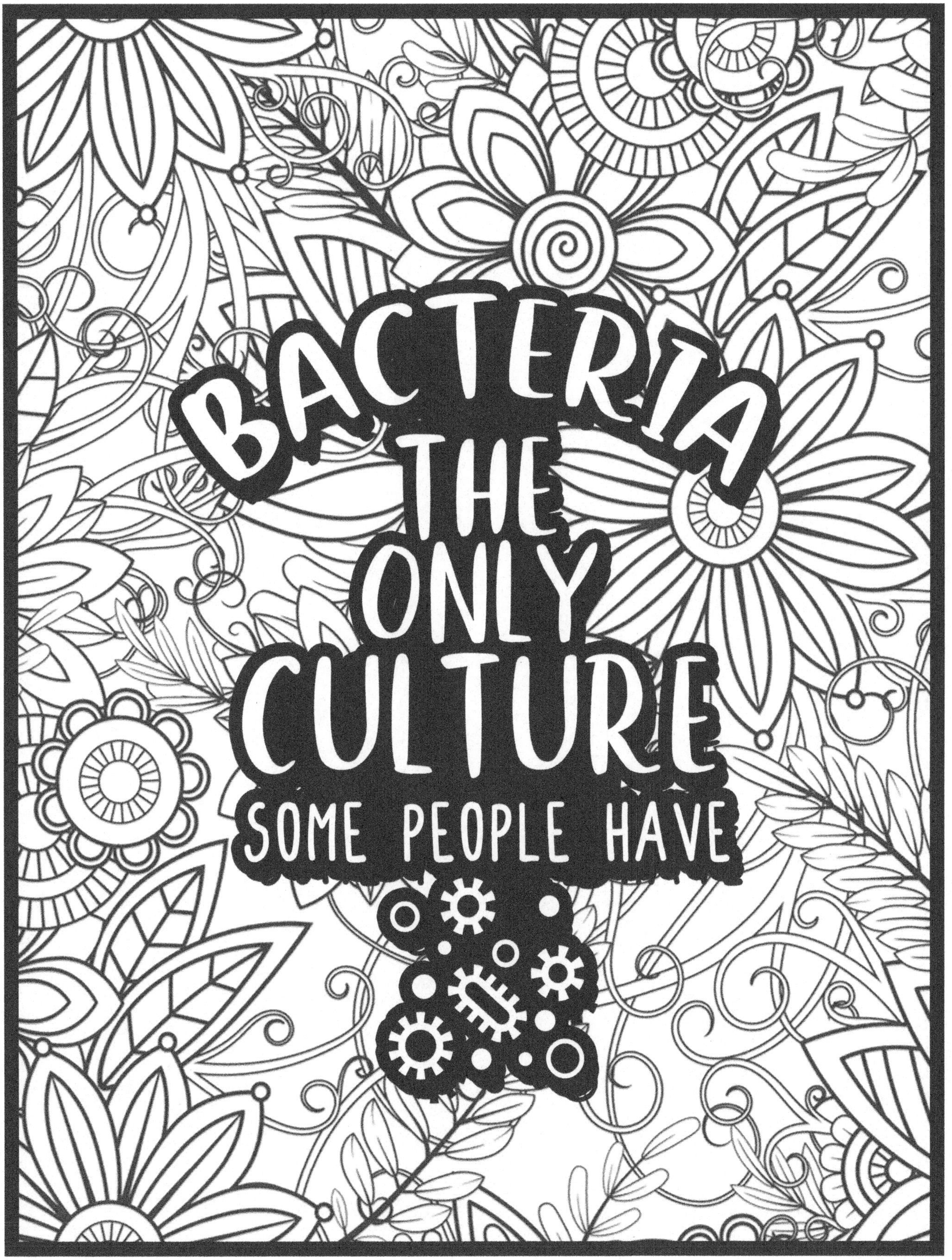
BACTERIA
THE
ONLY
CULTURE
SOME PEOPLE HAVE

I PLAY
WITH
BACTERIA

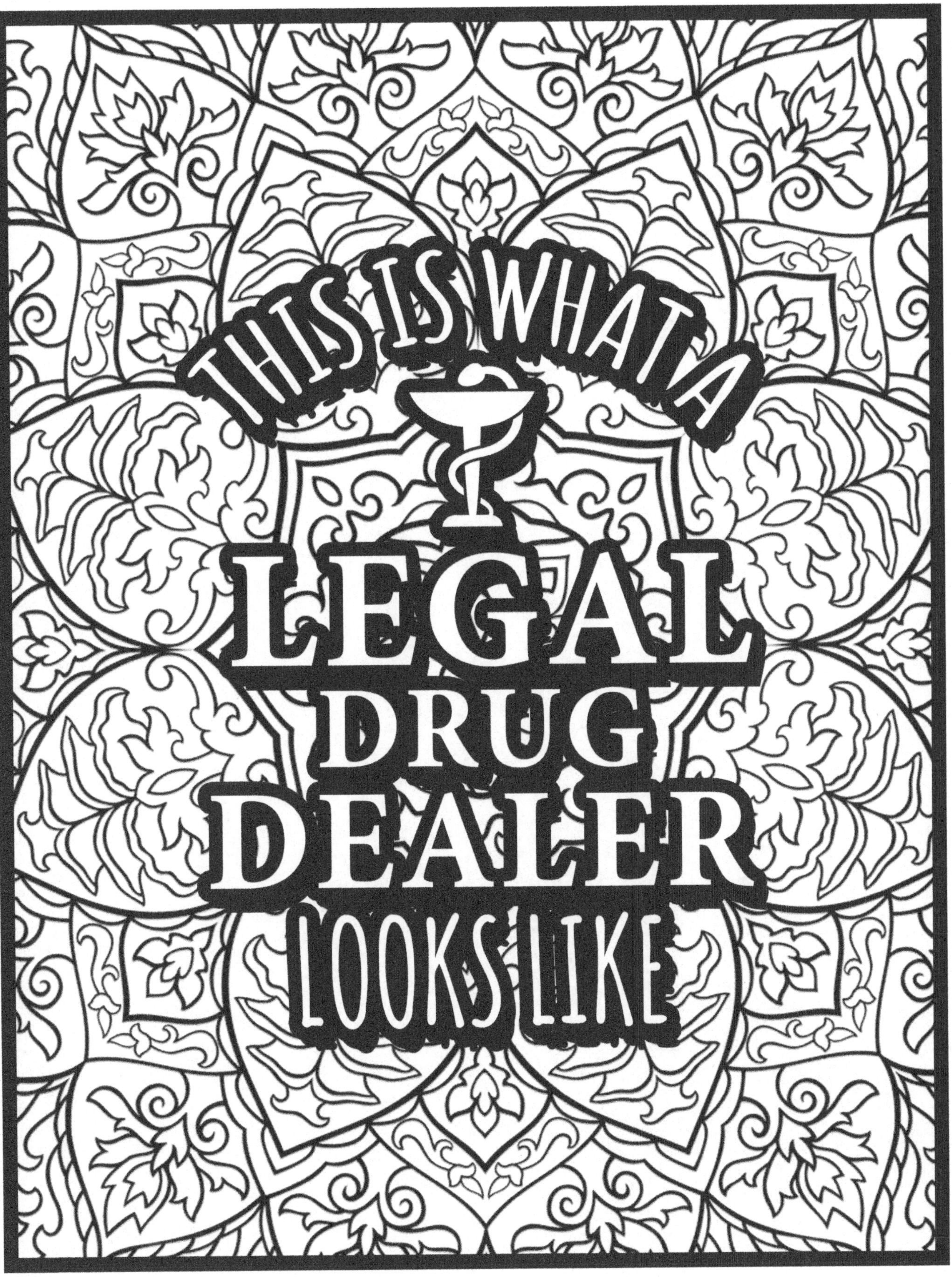
THIS IS WHAT A
LEGAL
DRUG
DEALER
LOOKS LIKE

I'M A
Pharmacist
WHAT'S YOUR
SUPER
POWER?

I'm A
PHARMACIST
To Save Time, Let's Just
Assume That I'm
NEVER
WRONG